DEVON LEGENDS

COMPILED BY JAMES WHINRAY

TOR MARK PRESS · PENRYN

'Tales such as these flutter round Devon
as plentifully as bats flit across the chimneys
of an ancient manor house.'

So wrote Arthur Norway in the 1890s, when legends were a
much livelier part of Devon culture than they are today.

We have collected these tales from many sources, among them
Mrs Bray, T H Cooper, Sabine Baring-Gould,
J H Harris, Robert Hunt, T H Moggridge, Arthur Norway,
J L W Page, Richard Polwhele, John Prince,
Mackenzie Walcott, Thomas Westcote and the
early volumes of the *Transactions of the Devonshire Association*.
They are generally told in the original form, lightly edited to
avoid archaic usage.
We hope you will enjoy them, and also our other volumes of
Devon and Cornwall folk-lore, which you will find listed overleaf.

The Tor Mark series

Folklore

Classic Cornish ghost stories
Classic Devon ghost stories
Classic West Country ghost stories
Cornish fairies
Cornish folklore
Cornish legends
Customs and superstitions in
    Cornish folklore

Demons, ghosts and spectres in
    Cornish folklore
Devonshire customs and
    superstitions
Devonshire legends
The pixy book

Other titles

Charlestown
China clay
Classic Cornish anecdotes
Cornish fishing industry
Cornish mining – at surface
Cornish mining – underground
Cornish mining industry
Cornish recipes
Cornish saints
Cornwall in camera
Cornwall's early lifeboats
Cornwall's engine houses
Cornwall's railways
Devonshire jokes and stories
Do you know Cornwall?
Exploring Cornwall with your car
Harry Carter – Cornish smuggler
Houses, castles and gardens in
    Cornwall

Introducing Cornwall
King Arthur – man or myth?
Lost ports of Cornwall
Old Cornwall – in pictures
The pasty book
Shipwrecks around Land's End
Shipwrecks around the Lizard
Shipwrecks around Mounts Bay
Shipwrecks – Falmouth to Looe
South-east Cornwall
The story of Cornwall
The story of the Cornish language
The story of St Ives
The story of Truro Cathedral
Tales of the Cornish fishermen
Tales of the Cornish miners
Tales of the Cornish smugglers
Tales of the Cornish wreckers

First published 1996 by Tor Mark Press,
Islington Wharf, Penryn, Cornwall TR10 8AT
© 1996 Tor Mark Press
ISBN 0-85025-349-7-355-1
The cover illustration is by Trevor Parkin
Printed in Great Britain by Burstwick Print and Publicity Services, Hull

The story of Queen Elfrida

Elfrida was the daughter of Ordgar, Earl of Devon, and a woman of great beauty. King Edgar came to hear of her beauty, but there were many beautiful women in the land so he sent his trusted young friend Earl Ethelwold to visit the Earl, and report back on his daughter. Earl Ethelwold found that Elfrida was so beautiful he could not bear that any other man should marry her, even his friend the king, and he sent back a report that, yes, she was attractive, but not as much so as they had been led to believe. Truly, the Earl was an important man, yet there were even better strategic marriage alliances the king might make. On the other hand, if the king was willing, he Ethelwold would find such an alliance extremely useful.

Trusting his friend totally, the king agreed. Ethelwold and Elfrida were married, and lived happily enough, until one day the king announced that he would be visiting them at their estate, near Buckland Monachorum. Ethelwold was terrified, for the king would immediately discover he had lied. He had only one recourse. He must tell his wife exactly what had happened, stressing that it was his extreme passion for her which had overcome his loyalty and his discretion, and begging her to make herself as unattractive as she could when the king arrived.

Elfrida listened, and said she entirely understood. When the king was due, she spent most of a day in her own quarters with her maids, and when she emerged to greet him she had never looked more beautiful, and never been more vivacious. King Edgar was entranced, and Earl Ethelwold appalled.

The next day they went hunting on the forest of Dartmoor, and King Edgar's boar spear pierced Ethelwold's heart in a hunting accident. Not long afterwards, Elfrida became queen. It is said that Elfrida haunts the ruins of Tavistock Abbey, wandering hither and thither in search of rest.

Ordulph

Ordgar, Earl of Devon, and his wife simultaneously had a vision in AD 961 which led them to found Tavistock Abbey, but he died before it could be completed. It was left to his son Ordulph to finish the work. This Ordulph was a man of gigantic stature and strength, who strode over streams ten feet wide with no need for jumping.

One evening, he was travelling towards Exeter with King Edward the Confessor. They came to the gates of the city and found them locked and barred. The porter, knowing nothing of their coming, was absent. Ordulph, leaping from his horse, took the bars in his hands and, with apparent ease, broke them in pieces, at the same time pulling out part of the wall. Not content with this, he gave a second proof of his strength: wrenching the hinges with his foot, he laid the gates open.

Topsham and Exeter

Until about 1300 the river Exe was navigable to Exeter, and legend states that as a result of what he saw as an affront by the city, Hugh Courtenay, Earl of Devon – or perhaps his wife the Countess, Isabella de Fortibus – blocked the river with obstructions, built the port of Topsham, and forced the merchants of Exeter to use the new facilities, taking goods to and fro by horse and cart and of course paying tolls for the privilege.

The cause of this vengeful action was three baskets of fish – the only ones to be found on a particular day in Exeter market after storms at sea had made fishing difficult. The Earl's caterer wanted all three; so did the Bishop's, and a quarrel arose. The Mayor had to decide the dispute, and he was aware that the citizens also wanted the fish. His compromise was one basket for the Earl, one for the Bishop, and the third to go into the market. It seems fair enough, but the Earl was furious. The Mayor was the Earl's own retainer, and when he next came to the city he summoned the man to report to him.

Only too well aware of the violent temper of his master, the Mayor arranged for his colleagues and a crowd of citizens to accompany him and if necessary give him aid. At the Earl's town house, the Mayor was conducted to his presence, and the door shut behind him. Finding that none of his reasonable explanations did anything to mollify the Earl, he took off an outer coat which he wore, which was the Earl's livery, and quit his service. The Earl fell into an even greater passion, and the crowd, hearing the row, knocked loudly on the door and demanded their Mayor. Several times they were denied, but their increasing clamour finally persuaded the Earl that he might himself be in danger, and he entreated the Mayor to calm the people, which he did. And although the Earl afterwards seemed to have been pacified, he ever afterwards sought means of revenge against the city.

The Doones of Bagworthy

In 1869, R D Blackmore's novel *Lorna Doone* was published, and promptly gave Exmoor publicity and notoriety. The story was at first thought to be his own invention, but a little guidebook to Lynton and Lynmouth, published about fifteen years earlier, reveals an older tradition. Whether Blackmore used this book as his inspiration, or had the story direct, is not known. Here is the old story:

Bagworthy, or Badgeworthy as it is called by the peasants, lies on the side of Brendon parish adjoining Somersetshire, and connected with this spot are various traditions of the doings of a daring and successful band of robbers called 'the Doones of Bagworthy' who seem to have taken up their residence there about the time of the Commonwealth. Situated among the extensive tracts of hills which surround Exmoor, far from the habitation of man, and until its enclosure in 1820 scarcely known to any but the half barbarous shepherd or the adventurous sportsman, stands the wood of Bagworthy.

Though still one of the favourite haunts of the forest deer, the stately natives of the glen and mountains, it has been decreasing in size for many years; and its boundaries half a century ago, as pointed out by some of the older shepherds, by far exceed its present dimensions.

The ruins of a village long forsaken and deserted stand in an adjacent valley, which before the destruction of the timber must have been a spot entirely suited to the wild inhabitant. Tradition relates that it consisted of eleven cottages, and that here the 'Doones' took up their residence, being the terror of the country for many miles around. For a long time they were in the habit of escaping with their booty across the wild hills of Exmoor to Bagworthy, where few thought it safe or even practicable to follow them. They were not natives of this part of the country, but having been stirred by the Revolution from their homes, suddenly entered Devonshire and erected the village alluded to. It was known from the first, to the inhabitants of the neighbouring parishes, that this village was erected and inhabited by robbers, but the fear which their deeds inspired in the minds of the peasants prevented them from attacking and destroying it. The idea is prevalent that before leaving home they had been men of distinction and not common peasants. The site of a house may still be seen on a part of the forest, called the Warren, which is said to have belonged to a person styled 'The Squire', who was robbed and murdered by the Doones.

A farm-house called Yenworthy, lying just above Glenthorne on the left of the Lynton and Porlock road, was beset by them one night; but a woman firing on them from one of the windows with a long duck gun, they retreated, and blood was tracked the next morning for several miles in the direction of Bagworthy. The gun was later found at Yenworthy, and purchased by the

Rev. WS Halliday. They entered and robbed a house at Exford in the evening before dark, and found there a child, whom they murdered; a woman servant who had concealed herself in the oven is said to have heard them say to the unfortunate infant the following barbarous couplet:

'If any one asks, who kill'd thee,
Tell them, 'twas the Doones of Bagworthy.'

It was for this murder that the whole county rose in arms against them, and going to their abode in great haste and force, succeeded in taking into custody the whole gang, who soon after met with the punishment due to their crimes.

Faggus and his strawberry horse

Faggus was a native of North Molton and by trade a blacksmith, but being engaged in a law suit with Sir Richard Bampfylde, he was ruined and obliged to leave his home. He then turned gentleman robber, and for many years collected contributions on the highways, sometimes with a companion named Penn, but more frequently alone.

Many stories are now told concerning his enchanted strawberry horse, that rescued him from all sorts of dangers, and it was chiefly by means of this horse that Faggus escaped punishment for so great a length of time.

On one occasion a large party of farmers agreed to ride home together from Barnstaple Fair, expressly for the purpose of avoiding an attack from Faggus, who was supposed to be in the neighbourhood. However, when they arrived at the post on the top of Bratton Down, Faggus rode up, a cocked pistol in each hand and the reins lying on the neck of his strawberry horse. He threatened them with instant death if they did not deposit their purses at the foot of the post. The farmers obeyed him in silent awe, and Faggus rode off with his booty.

He was once seized, while sitting in the alehouse at Simonsbath, but at his shrill whistle, his invaluable horse, having broken down the stable door, rushed into the house, and after seriously maltreating the enemies of his master with his hoofs and teeth, bore him off in triumph. On another occasion he was recognized in Barnstaple and closely pursued to the bridge, where he was met by a party of constables who blockaded the other end. Seeing all hopes of escape by the road completely cut off, he boldly put his horse at the parapet of the bridge. This he cleared, and swam off to the very great disappointment of his numerous assailants, who had considered his capture as now quite certain.

Intelligence being received at Exford that Faggus was to pass through that village on a certain day, a number of men were stationed in the road to endeavour to seize him. They had not been long at their post before Faggus rode up in complete disguise. 'Pray, my good friends,' said he, 'may I ask for what purpose you are waiting here in such numbers?' On being answered that they were waiting for Faggus, he replied that he knew him well for a great rascal, and volunteered his services in assisting to take him.

After a little more conversation he asked what firearms they had; four or five guns were produced. He proposed that they should be discharged and reloaded, to secure their going off when required, as the dampness of the morning might have injured the priming. This was agreed to, and when his advice had been taken and the guns were rendered temporarily useless, he produced his own pistols, and having declared his name and robbed his terrified adversaries, galloped away.

It being discovered on another occasion that Faggus had taken refuge in a house at Porlock, the whole of the inhabitants assembled; some seized the rusty arms which had long hung neglected over their chimneys, or been employed only in war against the timid wild fowl. Others armed themselves with scythes, pitchforks and other rustic weapons. They surrounded the house in a formidable array, shouting aloud, 'Faggus is taken! Faggus is taken!' But they were mistaken; the door suddenly opened and he rushed forth mounted on his strawberry horse, dashing through the crowd. Regardless of the shots and blows aimed at him from all sides, he disappeared, leaving them astonished and confounded at his daring and good fortune.

He was at length captured in an alehouse at Exbridge, in the following manner. One of the officers disguised as an old beggar woman entered the tap room where Faggus was. With his usual kindness he ordered the supposed vagrant some food and liquor, and sat down near 'her'. At a preconcerted signal, the disguised constable, rising quickly, pulled the chair from under Faggus and was immediately joined by others who had been concealed in the room; they instantly fastened Faggus' feet and hoisted him up to the bacon rack. The shrill whistle Faggus gave as was his custom when in difficulty was given in vain, for the poor horse had been shot in the stable at the very moment the attack was made upon his master.

All was now over with poor Faggus. He was tried and hanged at Taunton at the ensuing assizes.

Throughout his career not one act of cruelty was ever laid to his charge, whilst numerous are the acts of kindness and charity to the sick and the distressed, that are recorded of him. Like the celebrated Robin Hood, he seems to have taken from the rich to give to the poor, for it required but little to supply his own immediate wants, living as he did in the most frugal manner.

Childe

John Childe was a Plymstock man of large fortune, in the reign of Edward III. Having no children of his own, and being the last of his family, he made his will as follows, 'That wherever he should happen to be buried, to that church should his lands belong.'

It so happened a while after, that riding to the hunt in the forest of Dartmoor in a cold and sharp season, being in hot pursuit of his game, he chanced to lose his way and his companions, in a very bitter snow. Thus left in this wild and desolate place, this poor gentleman, exceedingly numb with cold, killed his horse, and having disembowelled him, crept into his warm belly for a little heat; which not being able to preserve him long, with some of his blood he thus further confirmed his will:

He that finds and brings me to my tomb,
The lands of Plymstock shall be his doom [reward].

And soon after, that same night, he was frozen to death.

After this sad accident, the snows being at length abated, some passer-by coming that way found Mr Childe there, frozen to death. Now some notice of the whole affair being brought to the monks of Tavistock, they came and fetched the corpse; and with all possible speed hastened to inter him in the church belonging to their own abbey.

This business was not so secretly carried out but that the parishioners of Plymstock had some intimation of it also. To forestall the design of the monks of Tavistock, they placed themselves at a certain bridge, which they conceived the corpse must necessarily pass, resolving to wrest the body out of their hands by force.

But they must rise betimes, or rather not go to bed at all, that will over-reach monks in matter of profit. The monks, apprehending themselves to be in danger of losing the precious relic, what do they do but circumvent the Plymstock men with a guile? For they presently cast a slight bridge over the river at another place, and so carried the corpse over and interred it, without ever inviting their Plymstock friends to the funeral. This thus done without resistance, these monks enjoyed the lands of Plymstock a long while after. In memory whereof, the bridge, which replaced their temporary structure, bears the name of Guile-Bridge (though more commonly Abbey Bridge) to this day.

The seven prebends

A poor inhabitant of Chulmleigh had many children and thought himself too much blessed in that kind; so, to avoid the expense that was likely to grow that way, he absented himself seven years from his wife; returning from this separation, and accompanying her as before, she was within a twelvemonth delivered of septuplets, all male, which made the poor man think himself utterly ruined. In despair, he put them in a basket and hastened to the River Exe intending to drown them. But divine providence following him, caused the lady of the land, Isabella de Fortibus, coming that instant in his way, to ask him what he had in his basket. He replied that he had puppies not worth the rearing. She asked to see them, intending to choose one for herself. Although he tried to put her off, she insisted. When she saw they were babies, she compelled him to acquaint her with the circumstances; when she had sharply rebuked him for his inhumanity, she immediately commanded that they should be taken from him and put to nurse, then to school; and when they became men, she provided a prebendship [a clerical sinecure] for each of them in the parish of Chulmleigh.

Sir John Fitz

Mr Fitz of Tavistock married a daughter of Sir John Sydenham. Immediately before the birth of the child who was to be his son and heir, Mr Fitz cast a horoscope to discover his child's future, and his calculations showed that, unless the birth could be delayed by one hour, the child would come to an unhappy end.

It proved impossible to delay the birth, and the prediction is said to have proved true. The boy succeeded to his father's estate and was knighted; owing to a dispute, he fought a duel in the year 1599 with his neighbour, Sir Nicholas Slanning of Bickleigh, and killed him, as tradition relates, under the gateway of Fitzford House. For this death Sir John procured pardon, but Slanning's widow brought her appeal in the Court of Queen's Bench and obtained part of his estate as damages.

Shortly after this, Sir John killed another person. On his way to court to sue again for pardon, he rested for a night at an inn in Salisbury. He was awoken from his sleep by a loud knocking at his chamber door and, fearing the ministers of justice were in pursuit of him, he seized his sword and in the dark slew the unfortunate person who had, by mistaking the chamber door, disturbed him. Lights were brought and Sir John found himself guilty for the third time of taking a life; fearing the penalty of his crimes, he stabbed himself to the heart.

The ghost of the black dog

There are many tales of black dogs, and of the pack of Wisht or Wish Hounds, as they are known on Dartmoor, or Yeth Hounds on Exmoor, which hunt the wild hills, often with the demon huntsman close behind them. Here is just one.

A man having to walk from Princetown to Plymouth took the road across Roborough Down. He started at four o'clock from the Duchy Hotel, and as he walked at a good swinging pace, he hoped to cover the sixteen miles in about three hours and a half. It was a lovely December evening, cold and frosty, the stars and bright moon, giving enough light to enable him to see the roadway distinctly zigzagged across the moor. Not a friendly pony or a quiet Neddy crossed his path as he strode merrily onward whistling as he went. After a while, the desolation of the scene seemed to strike him, and he felt terribly alone among the boulders and huge masses of gorse which hemmed him in. On, on, he pressed, till he came to a village where a wayside inn tempted him to rest a while and have just one nip of something short to keep his spirits up.

Passing the reservoir beds he came out on an open piece of road, with a pine copse on his right. Just then he fancied he heard the pit-pat of feet gaining upon him. Thinking it was a pedestrian bound for Plymouth, he turned to accost his fellow traveller, but there was no one visible, nor were any footfalls then audible. Immediately on resuming his walk, pit-pat, pit-pat, fell the echoes of feet again. And suddenly there appeared close to his right side an enormous dog, neither mastiff nor bloodhound, but what seemed to him to be a Newfoundland of immense size. Dogs were always fond of him, and he of them, so he took no heed of this, to him lovely, canine specimen. Presently he spoke to him, 'Well, doggie, what a beauty you are. How far are you going?' at the same time lifting his hand to pat him. Great was the man's astonishment to find no resisting substance, though the form was certainly there, for his hand passed right through the seeming body of the animal. 'Hullo, what's this?' said the bewildered traveller. As he spoke, the great glassy eyes gazed at him; then the beast yawned and from his throat issued a stream of sulphurous breath. Well, thought the man, I am in for it now! I'll just trudge on as fast as legs can carry me, without letting this queer customer think I am afraid of him. With heart beating madly and feet flying over the stony way, he hurried down the hill, the dog never for a moment leaving him or slackening its speed. They soon reached a crossway, not far from the fortifications, when suddenly the man was startled by a loud report, followed by a blinding flash as of lightning, which struck him senseless to the ground. At daybreak he was found by the driver of the mail-cart, lying unconscious in a ditch.

Tradition says that a foul murder was many years ago committed at this spot, and the victim's dog is doomed to traverse this road and kill every man he encounters, until the perpetrator of the deed has perished by his instrumentality. There are similar legends of the Black Dog throughout the county, and many wayside public houses have 'The Black Dog' for a sign.

The Devil at Widecombe Church

On 21 October 1638 the Church at Widecombe was struck by lightning and a terrible storm. There were several deaths; most dramatically a man's skull was shattered and his brains thrown upon the ground, while 'the hair of his head, through the violence of the blow, stuck fast to the pillar near him, where it remained a woeful spectacle a long time after.' The vicar distinguished himself by his calm handling of this terrible incident. Thus much is a matter of historical fact.

But needless to say, an explanation was needed, and it was clear that the Devil was involved.

'The agreement being out which the devil had made with some wicked youth, he had the power to seize him, even in the church, if he found him there sleeping. On his way through the churchyard, the Evil One overturned some boys he found playing at marbles upon the graves; and finding his victim sleeping in the pew as expected, he caught him up by the hair and dashed him against the moorstone pillar where the bloody evidence of his guilt and punishment, as it was believed, remained for a considerable period.'

Later it became clear that the Devil had been spotted on his way to the scene. Dressed in black and mounted on a black horse, he had enquired his way to the church from a woman who kept a little ale-house on the moor. He offered her money to be his guide, but she distrusted him on observing that the beer turned to steam as it went hissing down his throat.

Finally her suspicions were confirmed when she glimpsed a cloven foot, which the Devil can never keep concealed, even when he wears boots.

The snake doctor of Bow Bridge

There lived at Kilmington in days of yore a famous 'medicine man' called Bow, who possessed the secret of a never failing antidote to reptile poison. Among the means adopted to proclaim his healing skill was one as horrid as it was attractive and successful. At fairs and wakes it was his wont, when vending from a stage his famous nostrums, to allow himself to be stung by infuriated adders to the extreme of vital endurance, and, in a few minutes, to prove the efficacy of his marvellous antidote by appearing safe and sound before the wondering and delighted crowd. His fame spread far and wide, and very envious were his less successful rivals. Now it came to pass, on a wake day at Axminster, that while the 'doctor' was in preparation for this crowning feat, some heartless rascal picked his pocket of the precious antidote. The disgusting exhibition soon commenced. Some vipers were applied to his bare neck and arms, and they soon performed their part. The poor wretch prepared to apply the sovereign remedy. Horror of horrors, it could not be found. Only at his home, a mile and a half away, was there a store of his infallible preparation.

Too well he knew his dreadful fate, unless that home could be very quickly reached. His desperate situation gave him courage. Shrieking fearfully he pushed aside the astonished crowd and started at his topmost speed for Kilmington. But the poison gained upon him. It rushed through his boiling veins – it mounted to his brain – and while in the act of crossing what was then called Stoford Bridge he dropped, in awful delirium, upon a spot from which he never rose. Bow Bridge, so saith Tradition, received its name in commemoration of this event.

Daddy's Hole, Torquay

Long before Torquay existed, a proud and beautiful girl loved a knight of this district, but alas her love was not returned; he loved another. One evening she was wandering sadly along the coast when she met her rival, and in her anguish mistook a smile of happy innocence for one of contemptuous indifference. Scarcely knowing what she was doing, her anger and bitterness quite out of control, she hurried on, and reached the home of her rival just as the evening light was fading. In the quiet which prevailed, she suddenly heard the cry of hounds – no ordinary hounds these, but the dreaded Wish Hounds, which hunt far and wide across Devon, with the Demon Hunter not far behind them. And there before her were two of these savage hounds, their eyes red and glaring, and the Demon Hunter on his giant black steed. She fainted, as well she might.

When she revived, she found a young man bending over her, asking her how she was, and she asked him, very timidly, if he had seen or heard the Demon Hunter. He assured her he had not, but had come to that spot himself to bewail a disappointed hope, for the woman he loved would marry another, a richer, man. He begged her to trust him, and at last she told him the tale of her own love and the scorn of her rival. And it turned out that her rival was the very same young woman who had spurned the stranger.

'If I promise you revenge,' he said, 'will you pledge yourself to be mine?' And she promised to trust him, for he had a very handsome face, earnest but sad, and they met again the next evening, and the next. Night after night they walked over the fields and waste, where now there are but streets and gardens, and the mysterious stranger whispered words of love, and vowed most confidently that they should be together for ever, and at last he told her that her former love would meet the next night with her rival, and told her where, and that if she wanted revenge, then was the time to do it.

She acted upon his advice. She stole after them that night, and as the clouds scudded past the moon, she stabbed in her mad jealousy both the young man she had once loved and his betrothed. There on Daddy Hole Common the deed was done.

As the last breaths of the dying pair expired, a fearful storm arose. The very earth shook, and the stars and moon withdrew their light, but in the darkness could be seen the fiery nostrils of a steed, on which sat the dark stranger to whom the murderess had bound herself for ever. She tried to escape him, but in vain.

The Demon Hunter and his dreadful hounds pursued her and then seized her, and then bore her to the ground. The strong earth rocked and quaked. 'Mine, mine for ever!' shouted the demon, as the hot flames rose around them, and he, with his hounds and his prey, sank into an awful abyss below.

'Tis only fayther

Once upon a time a gentleman set out on horseback to cross Dartmoor, at the breaking up of a long and hard frost when the roads were only just beginning to be passable. Now though the thaw had begun, it had not yet melted the snow drifts as much as he had expected; he progressed only slowly, and towards evening it began to freeze again.

The mighty tors, which seemed to grow larger and taller as he paced forward through the dusk, gradually became enveloped with vapour and mist. The traveller did not know what to do.

To reach Tavistock that night would be impossible, as a fresh snowstorm was fast falling in every direction, and would add even further dangers to the way. To stay out all night on the cold moor, without shelter or food, must be certain death, and yet where was shelter to be found?

In this dilemma there was no point in standing still, so he paced onward, and at length he saw at a distance a certain dark object but partially covered with snow. As he drew nearer, his heart revived, and his horse, which seemed to understand all the hopes and fears of his master, pricked up his ears and trotted on, or rather slid on, a little faster. The discovery which had thus rejoiced the heart of man and beast was not only that of the dark object, but also a thick smoke which rose like a stately column in the clear frosty air from its roof, and convinced them that what they now beheld must be a cottage.

He presently drew nigh and dismounted, and the rap that he gave with the butt-end of his whip upon the door was answered by an old woman, who invited him in. He entered and beheld a sturdy peasant who proved to be the old woman's son, who sat smoking his pipe over a cheerful and blazing peat fire. The traveller's needs were soon made known, for in those days a gentleman expected his requirements to be met with little question by any peasant. An old out-house with a litter of straw accommodated the horse which, it is not unlikely, ate up his bed for want of a better supper.

The traveller felt very hungry and wanted a bed. Though there was but one bed beside the old woman's in the house, the son, who seemed a surly fellow, promised to give it up for the convenience of the traveller, adding that he would himself sleep that night in the old settle by the chimney corner. The good dame busied herself in preparing such food as the house could afford for the stranger's supper, and at length he retired to rest. Neither the room nor the bedding were such as promised much comfort to a person accustomed to the luxuries of polished life, but as most things derive their value from comparison, even so did these mean lodgings, when he reflected how narrowly he had escaped perhaps being frozen to death that night on the bleak moor.

Before going to rest he had observed in the chamber a large oak chest; it was somewhat curious in form and ornament and had the appearance of being of great antiquity. He made some remarks upon it to the old woman when she had lighted him upstairs, in order to see that all things in his chamber were as comfortable for his repose as circumstances would admit. There was something, he thought, shy and odd about the woman when he remarked on the chest, and after she was gone he had half a mind to take a peep into it, but he forebore and went to bed as fast as he could.

He felt cold and miserable; and who in that condition can ever hope for a sound and refreshing sleep? His was neither the one nor the other, for the woman and the chest haunted him in his dream, and a hollow sound, as if from behind his bed head, started him out of his initial sleep. As he started up in bed, the first thing he saw was the old chest that had troubled him in his dreams. There it lay in the silvery silence of the moonlight, look- ing cold and white and, as connected with his dream, a provok- ing and even alarming object of his curiosity. And then he thought of the hollow sound, which had seemed to call him from his repose, and the old woman's odd manner when he had talked to her about the chest, and the reserve of her sturdy son, and in short the traveller's imagination supplied a thousand subjects of terror; indeed so active did it now become that it gave action even to the most inanimate things; for he looked and looked again, till he actually fancied the lid of the chest began to move slowly up before his eyes!

He could endure no more. Starting from his bed, he rushed forward, grasped the lid with trembling hands, and raised it up at once. Who shall speak his feelings when he beheld what that fatal chest now disclosed? – a human corpse, stiff and cold, lay before his sight! So much was he overcome with the horror of his feelings that it was with extreme difficulty that he could once more reach the bed.

How he passed the rest of the night he scarcely remembered; but one thought, one fear, possessed and agonised his whole soul. He was in the house of murderers! he was the next victim! there was no escape; for where, even if he left the chamber, at such an hour in such a night, where should he find shelter on the vast, frozen and desolate moor? He had no arms, he had no means of flight, for if plunder and murder were designed, he would not be allowed to pass out of the house while the young man (now, in his apprehension, a common trafficker in the blood of the helpless) slept in the only room below, and through which he must pass if he stirred from where he was.

To dwell on the thoughts and feelings of the traveller during that night of terror would be an endless task. Rather let me has- ten to say that it was with the utmost thankfulness and not with- out some surprise that he found himself alive and undisturbed by any midnight assassin when the sun at last arose and threw the cheerful light of day across the monotonous desolation of the moor. He determined to hasten away, to pay liberally, but to avoid doing or saying anything to arouse suspicion.

On descending to the kitchen he found the old woman and her son busily employed in preparing no other fate for him than that of a good breakfast; and the son, who the night before was probably tired out with labour (and perhaps not all that pleased at the prospect of a night in the settle) had now lost what the gentleman had fancied to be a surly humour. He gave his guest a country salutation, hoped 'his honour' had found good rest, and proceeded to recommend the breakfast in the true spirit of honest hospitality; particularly praising the broiled bacon, as 'Mother was reckoned to have a particularly good hand at salting 'un in.'

Daylight, civility and broiled bacon the traveller now found to be the most excellent remedies against the terrors, both real and otherwise, of his imagination. The fright had disturbed his nerves, but the keen air of those high regions and the savoury smell of a fine smoking rasher, were great restoratives. Indeed so much did he feel reassured and elevated by the total extinction of all his personal fears that, just as the good woman was broiling him another rasher, he out with the secret of the chest, and let them know that he had been somewhat surprised by its contents, venturing in a friendly tone to ask for an explanation of so remarkable a circumstance.

'Bless your heart, your honour, 'tis nothing at all,' said the young man, ''tis only fayther!'

'Your father!' cried the traveller, 'What do you mean?'

'Why you see, your honour,' replied the peasant, 'the snaw being so thick, and making the roads so cledgey, like, when old fayther died two weeks agon, we couldn't carry 'un to Tavistock to bury 'un; so mother put 'un in the old box, and salted 'un in. Mother's a fine hand at salting 'un in.'

Need a word more be said of this sensitive traveller and his breakfast. He now looked with horror at the smoking rasher, and fancied it nothing less than a slice of old fayther. He got up, paid for his lodging, saddled his horse, and quitting the house where surprise, terror, joy and disgust had all by turns so powerfully possessed him, he made his way through every impediment of snow and storm.

Never afterwards could he be prevailed upon to touch bacon.

Sir Francis Drake

One day while Sir Francis Drake was playing a game of kales [nine-pins] on the Hoe at Plymouth, it was announced to him that a foreign fleet was sailing into the harbour close by. He showed no alarm at the news, but persisted in playing out his game. When this was concluded he ordered a large block of timber and a hatchet to be brought to him. He bared his arms, took the axe in his hand, and manfully chopped up the wood into sundry smaller blocks. These he hurled into the sea, when, at his command, every one arose a fireship; and within a short space of time, a general destruction of the enemy's fleet took place, in consequence of the irresistible strength of these vessels he had called up to 'flame amazement' on the foes of Elizabeth and England.

The people of Plymouth were so destitute of water in the reign of Queen Elizabeth that they were obliged to send their clothes to Plympton to be laundered in a fresh stream. Sir Francis Drake resolved to rid them of this inconvenience. So he called for his horse, mounted, rode to Dartmoor and hunted about till he found a very fine spring. Having fixed on one to suit his purpose, he gave a smart lash to the horse's side, pronouncing as he did so some magical words, when off went the animal as fast as he could gallop, and the stream followed on his heels all the way into town.

The innkeeper's daughter

When Parliament's troopers were in Tavistock during the Civil War, knowing that the innkeeper at the King's Arms was a royalist, they determined that his wine should not be used to drink healths to the king. The best way to prevent this seemed to be to wash it down their own throats, so that not a drop of ungodly wine should remain if the royalists retook the town.

But they started by clearing out all the food upstairs, which gave time for the innkeeper's daughter to form a plan. She was in the last stages of tuberculosis, or 'consumption', and of a wasted and ghastly appearance. She resolutely snatched up a white tablecloth and, thus attired, stole downstairs and took her post in the dingy confines of an old wine-cellar, at the extremity of a long, narrow, congested and ominously dark passage.

When she heard them making their way down the steps, she groaned a groan and stood still. The corporal who headed the marauding party stared towards the sound, and his eye caught the pale, thin, white and shadowy figure that, in a motionless attitude, stood with upraised and menacing hand at the back of the cellar.

'What the devil is that?' said one of the fellows.

'Devil or no devil, I will send a shot at the white mark,' said another. He raised his pistol and took a steady aim at the innkeeper's daughter. She neither moved nor spoke, such was her resolution.

'Do not fire,' said the corporal. 'The figure mocks thine attempts; do not strive with spirit, for yonder thing is neither flesh nor blood. Let us begone from this place, or something may happen.'

'Now I look again,' said the trooper, 'I see it is a ghost. The Lord have mercy upon us! I will sing a psalm!'

At hearing this the ghost was moved, and making as if she would advance upon the whole party, she sent every mother's son of them flying in fright. Up the steps they ran, much faster than they had descended. The cellar escaped rifling; the house was instantly abandoned; they didn't even stay to collect the booty they had already gathered above stairs.

The devil saves the Squire's skin

It is not unusual to hear in Devon of a man or woman selling their soul to the Devil, but a certain squire made a particularly strange agreement, that the Devil was entitled to his skin as well as his soul. The squire wanted a witness to the taking of his skin, since he did not want the rest of his body to be taken also, and over several bottles of particularly fine port had persuaded one of his neighbours to act as witness.

In due course the squire died and was buried in the family vault in the village church. After the funeral, the neighbour, now in a great state of alarm because the time of the flaying was set for that night, went to the parson and asked his advice.

The parson told him that there was no option but to keep his promise, but he should take with him a cockerel into the church. This he did, and he sat himself in the parson's pew, in case that was a bit holier than the other seats.

As midnight struck, the Devil appeared, prised open the grave, extracted the body and started the ghastly process. Then he held up the skin and with disgust commented that it hadn't been worth the effort, because it was full of holes. As he spoke, the cockerel suddenly crowed. The Devil started and looked round. In a great rage he pointed at the terror-struck man, and roared 'I'd have had your hide too if it wasn't for that bird you have there.'

The Devil's wooing

An old woman in the parish of Bridgerule, which is on the Cornish border, lived alone with her pretty daughter. One day, a carriage-and-four drew up on some pretext, and out stepped a fine gentleman, who was soon in deep and witty conversation with the girl. He left, but returned the next evening, and stayed longer. Before the evening was out, he had asked the girl to marry him, but she must agree to come away with him the very next evening. She was carried away by the attentions of this fine man, and agreed. Did she swear to come with him? Yes indeed.

But the girl's mother didn't like the man's fiery eyes, though she liked his coach and horses well enough, and she went to talk to the parson. The parson felt sure this must be the Devil. He advised her to take a candle and ask him, when he next came, to allow the daughter a little time, as long as it took for the candle to burn away, before she had to leave her home.

When the gentleman arrived to claim his bride, she asked for time to change into her best clothes, but only as long as it took the candle to burn down. As soon as the gentleman had agreed, and gone outside to wait in his coach, the old woman blew out the candle and rushed out of the back door to the parson, who promptly walled up the candle inside the church – where it still is today.

Of course, once the gentleman discovered how he'd been tricked, he was beside himself with rage, and drove off on the Tamerton Road. But some two miles short of North Tamerton, on Affaland Moor, the coach was seen to plunge into a bog in an explosion of blue flames.

Bideford Bridge

The site of Bideford Bridge was in dispute. The Virgin Mary wished to have it built where it stands, but the Devil wished to build it at the old ford, half a mile further up the Torridge. For a long time no progress was made, as every time the foundations were attempted by the Virgin Mary and her followers, the Devil came in the night and pulled them down.

At last it was decided to sink large packs of wool at the chosen place. Heavily weighted, these held so much rubbish and mud when the tide went out that the builders, under the direction of the Virgin Mary, built enough of the bridge to prevent the Devil being able to pull it down, so the bridge was successfully finished on the site chosen by the Virgin.

The Parson and the Clerk

Near Dawlish stand, out in the sea, two rocks of red sand-stone conglomerate, bearing these names. They are not the originals, which have long since worn away, but the story which attached itself to them was too good to be lost, so replacement rocks were found! Here is their story.

The Bishop of Exeter was sick unto death at Dawlish. An ambitious priest frequently rode with his clerk to make anxious enquiries after the condition of the dying bishop. It is whispered that this priest had great hopes of occupying the bishop's throne in Exeter cathedral.

The clerk was usually the priest's guide but somehow or other, on a particularly stormy night, he lost the road and they were wandering over Haldon. Excessively angry was the priest, and very provoking was the clerk. He led his master this way and that way, yet still they were on the elevated country of Haldon. At length the priest exclaimed in a great rage, 'I would rather have the Devil for a guide than you.'

Presently the clatter of a horse's hoofs was heard behind them and a peasant rode up on a moor pony. The priest told of his problem, and the peasant volunteered to guide them. On rode peasant, priest and clerk, and soon they were at Dawlish. The night was tempestuous, the ride had quickened the appetite of the priest, and he was wet through. Therefore, when his peasant friend asked him to supper, as they approached an old, ruined house, through the windows of which bright lights were shining, there was no hesitation in accepting the invitation.

There were a host of friends gathered together, a strange, wild-looking bunch of men. But as the tables were laden with substantial dishes, and black-jacks of beer or cider were standing thick around, the parson, and the clerk too, soon became friends with all.

They ate and drank, and became most irreligiously uproarious. The parson sang hunting songs, and songs in praise of a certain old gentleman with whom a priest should not have maintained any acquaintance. These in particular were highly appreciated, and every man joined loudly in the chorus. Night wore away, and at last news was brought that the bishop was dead. This appeared to rouse up the parson, who was only too eager to set to work to secure his ambition. So master and man mounted their horses, and bade adieu to their hilarious friends.

They were at the door of the mansion – yet somehow or other the horses did not seem disposed to move. They were whipped and spurred, but to no purpose.

'The devil's in the horses,' said the priest.

'I b'lieve he is,' said the clerk.

'Devil or no devil, they shall go,' said the parson, cutting his horse madly with his heavy whip.

There was a roar of unearthly laughter.

The priest looked round. His drinking friends were all turned to demons, wild with glee, and the peasant guide was an arch little devil, looking on with a marvellously curious twinkle in his eyes. The noise of waters was around them; and now the priest discovered that the mansion had disappeared, and that waves beat heavy on his horse's flanks, and rushed over the smaller horse of his man.

Repentance was too late.

In the morning following this stormy night, two horses were found straying on the sands near Dawlish; and clinging with the grasp of death to two rocks, were found the parson and the clerk. There today stand the rocks to which the devil has given the forms of the tall parson, and his clerk standing below and in front of him, an enduring monument to all generations.

The dragon of Cadbury

A fiery dragon was frequently seen flying between Cadbury Hill and Dolbury Hill in Broad Clyst, always by night, 'whereby it is supposed that there is great treasure hidden in each of them,' giving rise to the verse

If Cadbury Castle and Dolbury Hill dolven [dug] were,
All England might plough with a golden share.

Two stories of the barrows

In the words of Thomas Westcote (1630): A daily labouring man by the work of his hand and the sweat of his brow having gotten a little money, was desirous to have a place to rest himself in old age, and therefore invested it in some acres of waste land and began to build a house thereon, near a barrow named Broaken Burrow [in the parish of Challacombe, near Blackmore Gate] from which he fetched stones and earth to further his work. Having pierced into the bowels of the hillock, he found therein a little place, as if it had been a large oven, fairly, closely and strongly walled up; which comforted him much, hoping that there might be some treasure there hidden to maintain him more liberally and with less labour in his old years. Wherewith encouraged, he plied his work earnestly until he had broken a hole through this wall, in the cavity of which he espied an earthen pot, which caused him to multiply his efforts until he might make the orifice large enough to take out the pot, which his earnest desire made not long a-doing. But as he thrust in his arm and fastened his arm thereon, he suddenly heard, or seemed to hear, the noise of the trampling or treading of horses coming, as he thought, towards him, which caused him to forbear and arise from the place, fearing those coming would take his prize from him (for he had assured himself that it was treasure). But looking about every way to see what company this was, he saw neither horse nor man in view.

To the pot again he goes, and had the like success a second time; and yet, looking about, could see nothing. At the third time, he brought it out, and therein only a few ashes and bones, as if they had been of children or the like. But the man, whether by the fear (which yet he denied) or other cause which I cannot comprehend, in very short time after lost the sense both of sight and hearing, and in less than three months consuming, died.

Two men were encouraged by a peller or 'wise man' to break into a barrow, where they could expect to find treasure in a bronze cauldron. They tried to enlist the help of a fourth, since the peller was not strong enough to dig, and there was much work to be done. Their friend, however, had no stomach for the job. The peller warned the two diggers that they would feel extremely faint when they reached the bronze cauldron, but they must not allow themselves to be overcome, otherwise the treasure would disappear.

So they started digging, and in the centre of the barrow they found a stone chamber, and in the chamber they found the cauldron, covered with a stone. One of the men tried to lift the stone off the cauldron, but he felt faint, and asked the other to take his place, but when he tried, he too felt faint, and they both passed out.

When they came to, they consulted the peller, who told them that 'the birds were flown, and only the nest was left,' which they soon found to be true. They returned to the cauldron, and found the stone would now lift off easily, so they removed the cauldron. Inside it there was nothing at all, but the bottom of the cauldron, where the treasure should have been, was bright and clean, whilst the upper part was worn away with rust.

Temptation in the wilderness

One day, Bishop Brondescombe [Bishop of Exeter from 1258 to 1280] was riding over Dartmoor from Widecombe towards Bridestowe. There were no roads, and he and his retinue had laboured through bogs and almost despaired of reaching the edge of the wilderness. When they reached Amicombe Hill, they did not know which way to turn, for the bogs there are nasty. His attendants dispersed to seek a way. The bishop was overcome with fatigue and hunger. He turned to his chaplain and said, 'Our master in the wilderness was offered by Satan bread made of stone. If he were now to make the same offer to me, I doubt if I should have the fortitude to refuse.'

'Ah,' said the chaplain, 'and a hunk of cheese as well!'

'Bread and cheese I could not hold out against,' said the bishop. Hardly were the words out of his mouth when a moorman rose up from peat digging. He had a knapsack on his back.

'Master,' shouted the chaplain, 'dost thou chance to have a snack of meat with thee?'

'Yea,' replied the moorman, and approached them, hobbling, for he was apparently lame. 'I have some bread and cheese, but naught else.'

'Then give it to us, my son,' said the bishop, 'and I will repay thee.'

'Nay,' replied the stranger, 'I be no son of thine or of any proud churchman! And I ask no reward save that thou descendest from thy steed and takest off thy cap. Then salute me with the title of master and ask nicely.'

'I will do that,' said the bishop, smiling, prepared in his hunger to humour the fellow, and alighted. Then the moorman produced a loaf and a large piece of cheese.

The bishop was about to take off his cap and address the moorman in a tone of entreaty and by the title of master, when the chaplain perceived that the man had one foot like that of a goat. He instantly cried out to God, and pointed out to the bishop what he saw. In holy horror, the bishop made the sign of the cross, and lo! the moorman vanished but the bread and cheese remained, transformed to stone.

Drake scares the demons

When Sir Francis Drake was building a mansion out of the stones of Buckland Abbey, some supernatural force removed them to a great distance. This happened twice, before Sir Francis lost patience and determined to watch for his mysterious enemy. So he climbed into a tree. At midnight a troop of little devils ascended from the earth and with much merriment proceeded to raze the walls and remove the stones as before.

Once more the workmen built the walls and that night Sir Francis dressed himself in white and again mounted into his leafy shelter. Up came the devils as before, but when they approached the tree Sir Francis worked his arms and called 'Kikkeriki!' with all his might. Even devils have nerves, and this was too much. They fled in dismay, and so the mansion was built.

Smuggler's Leap

On the road from Lynton towards the hamlet of Martinhoe, at a point where it most closely approaches the sea, is a chasm called 'the Smuggler's Leap'. Many years ago, when running contraband was a regular part of Devon life, a smuggler was riding fast over these cliffs, pursued by a king's officer. The exciseman had a better horse, and gained rapidly on his quarry. As pursuer and pursued drew abreast of the chasm, they were neck and neck and the smuggler swerved to avoid the exciseman's grasp. The movement was too much for his tired horse, which stumbled and with a wild snort went over the brink. But the smuggler did not fall alone. As he felt himself going, he clutched wildly at his enemy, and they rolled into the abyss together. It is said their bodies were discovered by seaweed gatherers 'locked together in a vice-like grip which had hurled them to eternity.'

Combe Martin

The last Martin of Combe Martin lived in a moated house near the church, and the moat was spanned by a drawbridge. One day, his son went hunting but the chase was prolonged and he did not return. Thinking that the young man would have accepted the hospitality of another of the hunters, Martin ordered the drawbridge to be drawn up as usual. Late that night, the son returned, more asleep than awake but still riding hard; not noticing that the drawbridge was up he plunged headlong into the water, where the corpses of himself and his horse were found in the morning. Wild with remorse and grief, the father pulled down his house, and left Combe Martin for ever.

The crusader's revenge

Hugh de Bruière loved Lady Hester of the house of Ilsham, and she preferred him to his rival de Pomeroy. Both men were called to go crusading with King Richard the Lionheart, and Hugh gave Lady Hester a ring in token of his love, while she gave him a rosary. A year passed, and de Pomeroy returned. He told her that Hugh had been killed in a battle with the Saracens, and not long after he offered himself as her suitor and, since Hugh was dead, within a year she had accepted him.

On the very night of the wedding a ship dropped anchor in Torbay, a boat was lowered, and a knight was rowed ashore. Seeing a blaze of light at Ilsham, the knight asked a fisherman what was happening, and thus Hugh learned that de Pomeroy, to whom he had entrusted a message for his lady, had played him false.

The next morning, de Pomeroy's body was found floating in the Dart, pierced with a dagger. But this summary revenge did not appeal to the bride who had become a widow on her wedding night, and she would have nothing to do with Hugh, and returned his ring.

De Bruière was struck with remorse. He had killed his friend in haste, and had not won back his lady. To expiate his sins, he founded Torre Abbey. The lady found the abbey a place of great calm, and here she came to pray, but she pined and before long she died, and was buried here. De Bruière then took the vows himself, and he too was in time buried here. His stone coffin survives, but the buildings he knew have long crumbled to dust.

The mayor's dinner

The Mayor of Great Torrington, Henry Lee, had taken part in the rebellion of 1549. He thought he had got away with it when Sir Anthony Kingston, the Provost Marshal, accepted his invitation to dine. During the meal, Sir Anthony asked the Mayor to have a gallows made ready for the afternoon, when it would be needed, and the Mayor complied. When they had finished eating and drinking, Sir Anthony asked to see the gallows and asked the Mayor whether he thought it adequate for the job. 'Yes, indeed,' said the Mayor. 'Good,' said Sir Anthony, 'because it is for you. You have been a most active rebel.'

Exactly the same story is told both of Bodmin and St Ives. Either Sir Anthony enjoyed his little joke three days in a row, or – as is very common with such tales – an ancient story has attached itself to a place and person local listeners would know about. The story may even be much older than 1549.

Kent's Cavern

Sir Kenneth Kent, who was involved in the murder of the gay King Edward II at Berkeley Castle, retired to Devon where he found a less than enthusiastic welcome from Sir Harry Lacey, whose daughter Serena he loved dearly. Sir Harry, indeed, plotted his death. Kent was warned of this by Serena, and narrowly escaped to hide in the cavern which is now named after him.

A fisherman below saw her ascending to the cavern with a

lantern to join him in his flight. But neither was ever seen to come forth again, and many years afterwards it was rumoured that a bold man had penetrated those murky recesses and seen a rusted suit of mail, in which was no living form, but a pale shape hovered beside it.

The black monk of Lynton

There is a story of Lynton Castle (only there is now no castle there) that once upon a time a thousand and more years ago it was in the possession of the Lady Edith, who had a notoriously violent temper. A 'black monk' lived at the castle and had her ladyship under his thumb in most matters, but even he sometimes found life with Lady Edith a little too hot for comfort.

Lady Edith was the only daughter of Earl Sigvald, and she had been betrothed to her Norse cousin before his conversion. After he became a Christian, there was trouble, because Lady Edith was not prepared to be converted but insisted on worshipping the ancient gods.

Her betrothed, who was also an earl, wrote to her that on the first day of the new moon he would come to claim her, and her ladyship sent back a message which made him turn pale, then red, then pale again. He was a placid man, for those times, so he contented himself with hanging the messenger from a tree within view of her window.

Lady Edith was well versed in runes and incantations, and when the black monk revealed himself as the Devil, she entered into a pact with him, if only he would defend her castle against the earl her cousin. The black monk saved the castle, and the lady was even more under his thumb. One day, while Lady Edith stormed around in one of her rages, the bell was rung at the postern gate. The Lady Edith opened the wicket herself, and there stood a friar, beseeching a donation 'for the missionaries'. Now this was not a favourite cause with the lady, so she slammed the door in the holy man's face, and called upon the black monk to throw the wretch into the sea.

The holy friar instantly recognised who the black monk really was, and made the sign of the cross as soon as he appeared, which so angered the 'monk' that he rent the earth asunder, and the great cliffs heaved in pain, and the Valley of the Rocks was formed.

Then the black monk carried off the Lady Edith, and if you ever see their figures in the sky, scudding before the wind, you may know that there is anger in the sky and desolation before them on sea and land.

The highwayman monk

Not far from Dawlish, at a place variously called Lidwell, Lithewell or Lady-Well, there dwelt a monk with a mighty appetite for good food, and without the means to enjoy it. His remedy was to assume nightly the dress of a wayfarer, and to trudge the roads demanding 'Your money or your life,' from wealthy travellers. By day he would lure women to his chapel and, after robbing and murdering them, throw their bodies down a disused well. After the suppression of the monasteries, and of his chapel, the well was found to contain a large number of human bones, which it was affirmed were those of women and young children. The shadowy forms of the women are sometimes seen hovering over this spot, while the wailing cries of children fill the air.

For once there is some historical evidence to support the legend. Robert of Middelcote, priest, was found guilty on 28 March 1328 of raping Agnes, daughter of Roger the Miller, and of burgling Robert Rossel's house and robbing Walter Scoria and others on the highway betweenTeignmouth and Haldon Hill.

The cannon ball marriage

A lady of the Drake family of Ashe House was betrothed to a sailor but broke her troth during his absence on some distant voyage, and chose another bridegroom. The wedding feast had begun and all was going on quite cheerfully, when the door opened without hands, and everyone turned to see who was coming in. For a moment nothing entered; but when the attention of the whole company had been roused, a cannon ball made its appearance rolling gently along the ballroom floor. It rolled on steadily and slowly until it reached the feet of the faithless bride, when it stopped and rooted itself so firmly to the ground that the united strength of those present could not make it budge.

It was clear that this remarkable event was a portent demanding close attention, and the lady very wisely interpreted it as a gentle hint that she was using the absent sailor rather badly. It was not too late to repent; which she accordingly did, sending her new lover about his business, and herself waiting for him who had a better right to her.

In Somerset, the same tale was told of Combe Sydenham house, where the 'cannonball' was long preserved. It was most probably a meteorite.

The white bird of the Oxenhams

My dear Sir,

I give you, as well as I can recollect, the anecdote related to me, by a late respected Baronet of this county. He told me that, having read in 'Howel's Anecdotes' of the singular appearance of a white bird flying across or hovering about, the lifeless body of the different members of the Oxenham family immediately after dissolution, and also having heard the tradition in other quarters, wishing rather for an opportunity of refuting the superstitious assertion, than from an idea of meeting with anything like a confirmation; having occasion to come to Sidmouth, shortly after the death of his friend Mr Oxenham, who resided in an old mansion not now standing, and the place of which is occupied by the houses called Sidlands; he questioned the old gardener, who had care of the house, as to who attended his master when he died, as Mr Oxenham had gone there alone, meaning only to remain there a day or two. 'I and my wife, sir,' was the reply. 'Were you in the room when he expired?' 'Yes, both of us.' 'Did anything in particular take place at that time?' 'No, sir, nothing.' But then after a moment's pause, 'There was indeed something, which I and my wife could almost swear we saw; which was a white bird fly in at the door, dart across the bed, and go into one of those drawers; and as it appeared in the same way to both of us, we opened all the drawers to find it, but where it went to we could never discover.'

If I recollect rightly, the man on being questioned had not heard of the tradition respecting such appearances, and that he was not prepared from previous instruction to confirm the story seems more than probable, by his only mentioning it at second thought, as though he hardly supposed the Baronet's enquiry had reference to anything supernatural, and by his not more positively making the assertion, which it seems probable he would have done, had he any end to answer by making up the story.

The bells of Ottery

Pixies hate church bells, since these were intended to drive away evil spirits, a category in which the priests included the pixies. When the pixies heard that a new bell planned for Ottery would be heard as much as twenty miles away, they tried to destroy it.

They went in great numbers to the foundry, and there dropped dew into the bell-metal, so that it cracked when it was cast. But the priests dedicated the whole foundry to St Michael, so that the next casting was successful. Then the pixies lay in wait for the men taking the bell from the foundry, which had to be done on a succession of huge rollers. They mystified their eyes with a false landscape, so that instead of going towards Ottery St Mary, they headed towards the sea, and would have gone over the cliffs with the bell, if it had not been for an accident. One of the lay brethren trod on a thorn, and instead of cursing, he said 'God bless us and save us!' Whereupon the pixies fled and the men's eyesight was restored.

At last the great bell reached the tower and was hung, but the pixies tied the clapper with gossamer threads, so that when the ringer tried to test it, it made no sound at all.

'That's pixy work,' he said to himself.

Now the bishop and his retinue arrived to christen the bell, which was to be named Mary, and all the god-fearing parishioners came too, and even those who were not so god-fearing, chuckling among themselves about the bell that would not ring. But the bishop said, 'We will christen the bell, and it will speak by the power of the spirit.'

So its god-parents took hold of the rope, and the bishop sprinkled the bell, giving it its name and praying that it would drive away thunder, lightning, and all evil spirits and pixies from both the living and the dead in Ottery. The godparents pulled the rope and started the bell swinging, and it spoke, for the pixies' spell was broken.

Fitz's Well

Sir John Fitz was riding over the moor one day with his wife when they lost their way, were in fact pixy-led, and they floundered through bogs and could nowhere hit upon the packhorse track that, in those days of Queen Elizabeth, led across the moors from Moretonhampstead to Tavistock.

Exhausted and parched with thirst they came upon a crystal stream, dismounted and drank copiously of the water. Not only were they refreshed, but at once John Fitz's eyes were opened, the spell on him was undone, and he knew where he was and which direction he should take.

Thereupon he raised his hand and vowed he would honour that well, so that such travellers as were pixy-led might drink at it and dispel the power exercised over them by the pixies. The spring still flows and rises under a granite structure erected in fulfilment of his vow by John Fitz; it bears his initials and the date 1568 in raised figures and letters on the covering stone.

The Devil's little joke

One night a moorman was riding home from Widecombe Fair. He had made money and had then had something to keep out the cold, for the night promised to be one of tempest. As he started on his homeward way, the moon shone out occasionally between the whirling masses of thick vapour. The horse knew the way perhaps better than his master, and they had crossed the great ridge of Hameldon and were mounting towards a circle of upright stones – reputedly a Druid circle, where the stones are said to dance on Christmas Eve – when he heard a sound that startled him, a horn; and then past him swept without a footfall a pack of black dogs.

The moorman was not much frightened – he had taken too much Dutch courage for that – and when a minute after the black hunter came up, he shouted to him, 'Hey, huntsman, what sport? Give us some of your game.'

'Take that,' answered the hunter, and flung him something which the man caught and held in his arms. Then the mysterious hunter passed on. An hour elapsed before the moorman reached his home. As he jogged on, he wondered what sort of game he had been given. It was too large to be a hare, too small for a deer. Not once since his meeting with the hunter had the moon flashed forth. Now that he was at his door, he swung himself heavily from his horse and, still carrying the game, called for a lantern.

The light was brought. With one hand the fellow took it, then raised it to throw a ray on that which he held in his arm – the game hunted and won by the black rider of the moor. It was his own baby, dead and cold.

A will-o'the-wisp

In the parish of Broadwoodwidger is a field in which, it is asserted, a will-o'the-wisp is regularly seen.

The farmer's son was delicate yet in the haymaking time he joined in with the work and, despite his feeble lungs, in making sweet hay with the maidens. He over-exerted himself, burst a blood vessel and died. Ever since, a blue flame has been seen dancing in this field, and even on the top of the haycocks.

Jan Nokes and the Doctor

Jan Nokes was a quiet steady workman who lived in Totnes. One night he was favoured with a wonderful dream relating to Berry Pomeroy Castle. He knew every portion of the castle, inside and out, and in the dream he found himself wandering through the ruins and impelled by some unaccountable attraction to examine very closely the chimney of one of those enormous fireplaces which are to be found in old mansions. A short way up the chimney he noticed a peculiar spot. In his dream, he removed the mortar and there was revealed to his astonishment a crock of gold.

The next morning Jan related the dream to his wife. Strange to say, the dream was repeated the following night, identical in every particular. Rising from his bed, he would have gone at once to the spot indicated, but yielded to his wife's prayers to leave it until another more suitable time. On the third night the dream was again repeated, and this time without disturbing his wife's sleep he dressed and felt his way out of the house in the dark. It was midnight, the rain descended in torrents and the wind blew so hard that Nokes had some difficulty in making his way down Fore Street against it, On approaching the bridge, he was met by a man on horseback. A solitary pedestrian in the street at such an hour in such weather was unusual, and Jan was not surprised that the horseman drew up and demanded who he was and where he was going. The worthy burgess was a certain Dr Sawbones, returning from a professional visit.

'Hallo! Who are you?'

'Well, I be Jan Nokes.'

'Jan Nokes! Why, what on earth calls you away at such a time of the night as this?'

'Well, doctor, I be gwain to Berry Castle.'

'What, to Berry Castle in this weather and at this hour! What can be your business there?'

Thus brought to the point, Jan related his dream fully and faithfully, and the remarkable way it had been repeated on three successive nights. Dr Sawbones appeared to be much struck by the earnest manner in which Nokes told his tale, but when it was over he insisted that it could be nothing more than a heated imagination, and strongly urged Jan to go back to his bed, adding, 'At all events, if you still think there is something in it in the morning, you can go to the castle then and make an examination by daylight.'

Thanking the doctor for his good advice, poor Jan retraced his steps and once more went to bed. But he was up early in the morning, the dream still vividly impressed on his mind, and he headed at once for the castle in order to solve the mystery. Directing his steps to the particular chimney in question, he at once perceived the exact spot which had been so clearly revealed to him in his dream.

He looked eagerly up, but in preparing to climb he stepped on some clods of dry mortar. His suspicions were aroused, and kicking the mortar aside, to his intense disgust he found that the place he had seen in his dream – the receptacle of the crock of gold – had been broken into. There was a cavity in the wall, but the crock had disappeared.

Jan Nokes to the day of his death believed that Dr Sawbones, after leaving him on Totnes Bridge, went to the castle himself and appropriated the treasure. He was confirmed in this belief by the fact that the doctor, previously in needy circumstances, afterwards seemed to possess considerable wealth, and laid the foundation of a rich family.

Cutty Dyer

The River Yeo at Ashburton is liable to 'freshets' or flash floods. At night, before the bridge was built, it was crossed on stepping stones, which depended on nerve and sobriety. The task was made much more difficult by an ogre called Cutty Dyer, who lay in wait for drunkards crossing the stream. He was described by people who saw him as being very tall, standing in the water to his waist, with red eyes as large as saucers, endeavouring to pull them into the water. When the stream was bridged, Cutty remained only to frighten little children into obedience, and he disappeared altogether when the streets were lit.

The night of the long knives

The Danes at one time held Hembury Castle, and the area around Buckfastleigh and Holne. They were only a raiding party, without their womenfolk, and they got hold of Saxon women when they could. They were such strong fighters that the Saxons could not drive them out, and a number of Saxon women decided to achieve what their men could not. They let themselves be 'surprised' and taken by the Danes, and that night at a given signal each one cut the throat of the man who lay with her. The Saxon men made an attack at the same time, so the castle was taken, which is how the Danes were got rid of at last.

'It is your choice to believe these stories or no.'
Thomas Westcote

THE END